Learning About Amphibians

By
DEBBIE ROUTH

COPYRIGHT © 2002 Mark Twain Media, Inc.

ISBN 1-58037-188-4

Printing No. CD-1534

Mark Twain Media, Inc., Publishers
Distributed by Carson-Dellosa Publishing Company, Inc.

The purchase of this book entitles the buyer to reproduce the student pages for classroom use only. Other permissions may be obtained by writing Mark Twain Media, Inc., Publishers.

All rights reserved. Printed in the United States of America.

Table of Contents

Introduction 1

Invertebrates and Vertebrates 2

An Internal Affair 4

What Is an Amphibian? 6

Herpetology: "Crawling Things" 8

Ancient Amphibians: The History of Amphibians 10

Classification 12

Classification of Amphibians: Amphibian Orders 15

Order Anura: Frogs and Toads 20

Amphibian Behavior 23

Metamorphosis: How Frogs Develop 26

Grow Up, Tadpoles!: Observation Activity 29

The Color of Frogs: Amphibian Observation Activity 32

Keeping an Eye to the Future: Disappearance of the Cascades Frogs 33

Where Did All the Frogs Go?: Creative Writing Assignment 35

Can Endangered Amphibians Recover? Conservation/Research 36

Amphibian Vocabulary: Study Sheet 37

Amphibians: Crossword Puzzle 38

Reviewing Key Concepts: Amphibian Jeopardy 39

Amphibians: Unit Test 41

Answer Keys 43

Bibliography 46

Introduction

Welcome to a series of books devoted to the Phylum *Chordata*. A **chordate** is an animal that has a **spine** (backbone), which is made up of small bones called **vertebrae**. Most chordates have specialized body systems and paired appendages; all at some time have a notochord, a dorsal nerve cord, gill slits, and a tail.

Every animal in the animal kingdom can be subdivided into two main groups. The **invertebrates** (without backbones) make up 95 percent of all the known animals. The **vertebrates** (with backbones) make up only five percent of the animal kingdom. The vertebrates (chordates) are then divided even further into seven groups called classes—jawless fish, cartilaginous fish, bony fish, amphibians, reptiles, birds, and mammals. Each class has special characteristics all its own.

This book is devoted to the special **class** (group) of vertebrates called **amphibians**. The word *amphibian* comes from the Greek word *amphibios,* which means "double life." They are well named, for amphibians are vertebrates that spend part of their lives in water and part of their lives on land. Amphibians have thin, moist skin; most have lungs and a three-chambered heart; many undergo metamorphosis. The class *amphibia* includes frogs, toads, salamanders, newts, and caecilians.

Student observers will use many scientific process skills to discover the world of frogs, toads, newts, salamanders and caecilians—their habitats, behavior, and natural history. The reinforcement sheets that follow the lessons contain at least one higher-level thinking question. So, student observers, put on those thinking caps and use your process skills to observe, classify, analyze, debate, design, and report. This unit contains a variety of lessons that will help you practice scientific processes as you make exciting discoveries about these remarkable and changeable creatures called amphibians.

* **Teacher note:** Each lesson opens with a manageable amount of text for the student to read. The following pages contain exercises and illustrations that are varied and plentiful. Phonetic spellings and simple definitions for terms are also included to assist the student. The lessons may be used as a complete unit for the entire class or as supplemental material for the reluctant learner. The tone of the book is informal; a dialogue is established between the book and the student.

Invertebrates and Vertebrates

The animal kingdom is made up of more kinds of **organisms** (living things) than the other four kingdoms. Scientists **classify** (group) animals into two large groups. One group is made up of animals that have a backbone. The other group is made up of animals without a backbone.

Invertebrates

An **invertebrate** is an animal that doesn't have a backbone. This is by far the largest group of animals. The invertebrates make up 95 percent of all the known animals. Scientists have already given names to over one million species of invertebrates. Invertebrates have an **exoskeleton** (skeleton on the outside) or no skeleton at all. The exoskeleton is on the outside of the body and is made up of a hard, waterproof substance called **chitin**. The exoskeleton protects and supports the body. Some invertebrates must **molt** (shed) their exoskeleton in order to grow. A grasshopper may molt seven times in order to reach adulthood. There is always a reason for everything an animal does. Most of an animal's behavior has something to do with the three basic needs. Every animal needs food, oxygen, and shelter. An animal can only stay alive if it has food and water to eat and drink, oxygen to breathe, and shelter for protection from weather and enemies. When you are watching invertebrates, can you guess why they do the things they do?

Invertebrate animals include sponges; corals and jellyfish; worms; starfish and sea urchins; mollusks, such as snails and octopuses; and arthropods, such as insects, spiders, and crabs.

Vertebrates

A **vertebrate** is an animal that has a backbone. A **backbone** consists of a spinal column and a **cranium** (brain case). The vertebrates are the smallest group of animals. Only five percent of the known species of animals are vertebrates. Vertebrates live in water as well as on land. They are the most complex organisms in the animal kingdom. They are also the most familiar of all the animals. The largest animals on earth are vertebrates. Vertebrates can grow very large because they have an **endoskeleton** (skeleton on the inside of the body). The endoskeleton does not limit the growth and size of the animal. The endoskeleton covers and protects the soft body parts. It gives shape to and supports the animal's body. Vertebrates include fish; amphibians, such as frogs and toads; reptiles, such as snakes and lizards; birds; and mammals. In fact, you are a vertebrate.

Name: _____ Date: _____

Invertebrates and Vertebrates: *Reinforcement Activity*

To the student observer: Do you know the difference between an invertebrate and a vertebrate?

_____

_____

Analyze: Identify the characteristic that divides the animals into two large groups.

_____

_____

Directions: Answer the following questions.

1. What two groups make up the animal kingdom? _____

    _____

2. What is the difference between a vertebrate and an invertebrate? _____

    _____

    _____

3. Which group is the most familiar group? _____

4. Which group is the largest group? _____

5. Which group do amphibians belong to? _____

6. What is an exoskeleton? _____

    _____

    _____

7. What is an endoskeleton? _____

    _____

    _____

8. What is chitin? _____

    _____

9. What must an invertebrate do in order to grow? _____

    _____

10. What are three basic needs all animals have? _____

    _____

    _____

© Mark Twain Media, Inc., Publishers

An Internal Affair

The Backbone

The backbone or spine is a long column of bones called **vertebrae** that run along the animal's back. The spine connects to the **cranium** (brain case). Most vertebrates have vertebrae made of bones. Some have vertebrae made of cartilage. You can feel your vertebrae by running your hand down the back of your neck and between your shoulder blades. The row of hard, bony lumps runs all the way down to your bottom. This is your backbone.

When you touch a hot pan, your nerves relay a message to your brain, telling you that you are feeling pain.

The backbone has a very important job to do. Every vertebra has a hole in the middle and is joined to the next by a pad of **cartilage** (KART ul idj). Cartilage is a soft, flexible tissue that is rubbery and cushions the bony vertebrae. The backbone is like a hollow, flexible tube. Through the middle of the tube runs the spinal cord. The **spinal cord** (a thick bundle of nerves) receives and sends messages from the brain. The spinal cord also receives messages from the animal's body and carries the information to the brain. The brain interprets this information and sends messages back to the rest of the body. Imagine how busy the nerves in your backbone are. Thousands of messages rush along them every second. The backbone protects this passageway of nerves. The **nervous system** is made up of the brain, the spinal cord, and nerves. The animal's nervous system controls all body activities. If the spinal cord is damaged, the messages can't get through from the nerves to the brain or from the brain to the nerves. Sometimes, if an animal injures its back, it can't move certain parts of its body.

The Skeleton

Some animals do not have a skeleton; their bodies are soft. Other animals have a skeleton on the outside of the body called an exoskeleton. The animals we are studying in this unit have a skeleton on the inside of the body, called an **endoskeleton**.

The skeleton makes a framework that supports and shapes the animal's body. The skeleton affects the way an animal moves. The bones work together with muscles to move the body. Another job of the skeleton is to protect organs. For example, the ribs protect the lungs. Do you know what the skull protects?

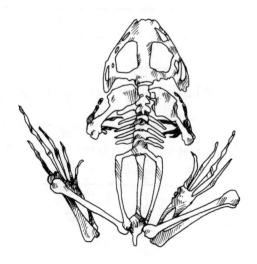

© Mark Twain Media, Inc., Publishers   4

Name: _____ Date: _____

An Internal Affair: *Reinforcement Activity*

To the student observer: Can you imagine how busy the nerves in your backbone are today? Can you name one message your brain received during the past hour?

_____

_____

Analyze: Nerve cells do not reproduce themselves like other body cells. What might happen if all the nerve cells in your feet were destroyed?

_____

_____

Directions: Answer the following questions.

1. What is the backbone, and what does it do? _____

_____

_____

2. What are the main parts of the backbone? _____

_____

_____

3. What is the spinal cord, and what does it do? _____

_____

_____

4. What happens when the spinal cord is damaged? _____

_____

5. What is the nervous system, and what does it do? _____

_____

_____

_____

6. What is the skeleton, and what does it do? _____

_____

_____

_____

What Is an Amphibian?

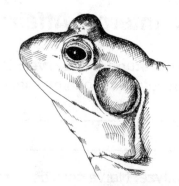

Kingdom: *Animalia*
   Phylum: *Chordata*
      Subphylum: *Vertebrata*
         Class: *Amphibia* (am FIB ee uh)
            Means "double life"

    Amphibians are a class of vertebrates. Vertebrates are animals that have a bony internal skeleton built around a backbone. Amphibians are **ectothermic** (cold-blooded) just like fish and reptiles. They cannot produce their own body heat the way warm-blooded animals can. If the temperature around them is cold, the amphibian becomes cold and lazy. The amphibian's body functions slow down.

    The name *amphibian* means "double life." This refers to the fact that they live part of their lives in water and part of their lives on land. The **tadpoles** (young forms) have gills and must live in water. The adult forms have lungs and may live on land. Lungs allow an animal to take in oxygen from the air. Frogs go through a life cycle called **metamorphosis**. Metamorphosis is a change of form from egg to tadpole to adult frog.

    Have you ever picked up an amphibian? The skin of most amphibians is soft and moist. Toads, however, have dry, rough skin covered with bumps that look like warts. Amphibians usually feel sticky to the touch. Many amphibians have a thick, slimy substance called **mucous** that keeps the skin moist. Some amphibians have special glands, called parotoid glands, that secrete a poisonous substance. Because their skins are not waterproof and cannot hold in moisture, they are usually found in moist places. Amphibians can absorb oxygen through their skins.

    Amphibians must return to water to mate and lay their eggs. Amphibian eggs are called **spawn**; they do not have a shell and would dry out if they were laid on land. The females of most toad and frog species lay hundreds of eggs at once. Frogspawn is laid in one big mass; toadspawn is laid in long strings. Other female amphibians lay their eggs one at a time beside underwater plants.

    There are about 3,000 different species of amphibians. Living amphibians are divided into three **orders** (groups) based on their body structures: frogs and toads; salamanders, sirens, and newts; and the odd caecilians (see SIL ee uns).

Salamander

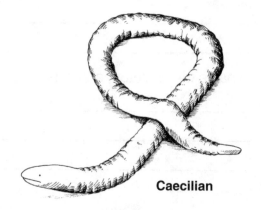

Caecilian

© Mark Twain Media, Inc., Publishers

Name: _____ Date: _____

What Is an Amphibian?: *Reinforcement Activity*

To the student observer: What characteristics of amphibians can you identify?

_____

_____

Analyze: Which amphibian characteristics explain why amphibians need a moist habitat?

_____

_____

_____

1. Solve the puzzle below:

    A _____   A/An _____ is an animal that lives part of its life in water and part on land.

    M _____   Amphibian _____ "double life."

    P _____   Amphibians belong to the Chordata _____.

    H _____   Frogs do not produce their own body _____.

    I _____   Vertebrates have a bony _____ skeleton.

    B _____   Amphibians are grouped according to their _____ structures.

    I _____   When an amphibian gets cold, everything going on _____ its body slows down.

    A _____   _____ are a class of vertebrates.

    N _____   Frogs _____ a moist habitat.

    S _____   Most amphibians produce a slimy _____ called mucous.

2. Answer the following questions.

    a. What are the three groups of amphibians? _____

    _____

    b. Name four characteristics of amphibians. _____

    _____

    _____

    _____

Herpetology: *"Crawling Things"*

Scientists used to think amphibians and reptiles were closely related, so they **classified** (grouped) them together. Scientists today realize that while they look very much alike on the outside, on the inside they are very different. Scientists have studied live specimens and dissections of both classes. Because of these studies, we now know amphibians are not reptiles. Amphibians have no scales, can breathe through their moist skin, and need to return to water to lay their unprotected eggs. Scientists also discovered that amphibians develop differently; they must go through metamorphosis. **Metamorphosis** is a change in development as the young amphibian grows from an egg to a larva to an adult. Reptiles do not go through metamorphosis. When reptiles hatch, they are exact images of their parents.

Both classes are vertebrates, and both are ectothermic, which means that they obtain heat from outside sources. They must move to warmer or cooler surroundings as the need arises. Cold-blooded (ectothermic) animals have an advantage over warm-blooded (endothermic) animals because they do not have to maintain a constant body temperature for their survival. This allows amphibians to be able to go for long periods of time between meals.

In some cold climates, the amphibian adjusts to its surroundings by hibernating. The state of **hibernation** is when an animal's body functions slow down; the entire body becomes at rest. It will remain in this state and live off its body fat until warmer conditions return. In some climates, such as the hot desert, an amphibian may find the need to escape the extreme heat and dryness by **estivating**. This is very similar to hibernating except the animal finds a cool spot and slows down all body functions until cooler conditions return. Warm-blooded animals' body temperature remains constant no matter what the surrounding temperatures are like. They usually do not need to hibernate or estivate like cold-blooded animals.

Herpetology is a branch of science that deals with both amphibians and reptiles. The name of this science comes from the Greek word, *herpeton,* which means "crawling things." Herpetologists study all aspects of amphibians and reptiles. They are very involved with the conservation and protection of these animals.

Malaysian Leaf Frog

Horned Frog

© Mark Twain Media, Inc., Publishers

Name: _____ Date: _____

Herpetology: *Reinforcement Activity*

To the student observer: What is herpetology? _____

_____

Analyze: Why do modern scientists believe reptiles and amphibians belong in different classes (groups)?

_____

_____

_____

1. Why were amphibians and reptiles grouped together? _____

   _____

2. What are ectothermic animals? _____

   _____

   _____

3. What is an endothermic animal? _____

   _____

   _____

4. What advantage does a cold-blooded animal have over a warm-blooded animal?

   _____

   _____

   _____

5. What is hibernation? _____

   _____

   _____

6. What does it mean if an animal estivates? _____

   _____

   _____

7. What is metamorphosis? _____

   _____

   _____

Ancient Amphibians: *The History of Amphibians*

Ancestors

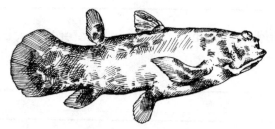

Lobe-finned fish

Some scientists believe the first amphibians appeared on Earth during the Devonian period. They have hypothesized that the first vertebrates to settle on land were amphibians. These scientists believe the ancestors of amphibians were a group of fish called lobe-finned fish. The lobe-finned fish developed bony supports for their fins and lungs for breathing air. The fleshy-lobed fins looked like legs and allowed them to haul themselves out of water and onto land. On land, they found new sources of food, mostly spiders and insects, and fewer enemies to prey on them. These are believed by some to have developed into early amphibians, such as the *"Ichthyostega"* (IK thee oh STEG a), which flourished on the land.

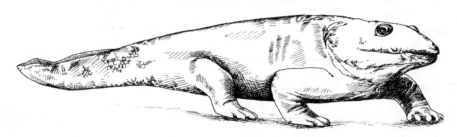

Ichthyostega

Ancient Amphibians

The oldest amphibian fossils show they were more varied in size and shape than they are today. The fossils show they had many features related to living on land. Their skeletons had a hip and shoulder girdle to support limbs. The skull was separated from the rest of the back, indicating a flexible neck. These amphibians had ears that could hear in air, eyelids to keep their eyes moist, and tongues to moisten and move food. Some ancient amphibians, such as the *Mastadonasauras,* were huge animals over 6 feet long. These ancient amphibians ruled the land until the dinosaurs overcame them. Only a few species survived to become the modern amphibians of today.

Modern Amphibians

Today's modern amphibians are smaller and less varied than the ancient amphibians, but they are still dependent on water for their survival. Most amphibians need water for their moist, scaleless skin and their shell-less eggs. The young amphibian starts life in a larva stage called a **tadpole**. The young larva breathes with structures called **gills** before it goes through a series of changes to become an adult. The adult carries on respiration by obtaining oxygen through its lungs and moist skin.

© Mark Twain Media, Inc., Publishers

Name: _____ Date: _____

Ancient Amphibians: *Reinforcement Activity*

To the student observer: Which animals do some scientists believe to be the ancestors of amphibians?

_____

Analyze: Frogs from the sky? Have you ever heard the expression "it's raining frogs"? What do you think led to the development of such an expression?

_____

_____

Directions: Complete the following questions.

1. Scientists believe _____ _____ are the ancestors of amphibians.

2. Fossils indicate that amphibians first appeared on Earth during the _____ period.

3. What are two reasons early amphibians flourished on land?

   a. _____

   b. _____

4. How are modern amphibians different from their ancestors? _____

   _____

   _____

5. What are three adaptations the ancient amphibians had for living on land?

   a. _____

   b. _____

   c. _____

6. Why are amphibians dependent on water? _____

   _____

   _____

   _____

7. How do young amphibians differ from adult amphibians? _____

   _____

   _____

Classification

The Science of Taxonomy

Classification is grouping things according to their similarities, or how they are alike. There are about 1.5 million different kinds of **organisms** (living things). Each year the list of living things grows longer. Scientists needed a way to keep track of so many organisms, so they developed a system of classification. The science of classification is called **taxonomy**. Scientists who group newly-discovered organisms are called taxonomists. I think the sorting of life would be quite a taxing business, don't you?

Early Classification

Aristotle, a Greek philosopher, developed the first classification system. Aristotle tried to group all living things into two huge groups, the plant kingdom and the animal kingdom. A **kingdom** is the largest category. Aristotle then divided the animals into smaller groups based on where they lived. Animals that lived on land were in one group, animals that lived in water were in another group, and flying animals went into a third group. You're probably already beginning to see a problem with this system. Aristotle's system had too many exceptions. What about frogs that spend their early years living in water and their later years living on land? They did not clearly fit into either group.

Classification Today

Carolus Linnaeus created a system that is still widely used today. He too grouped all the organisms into two main kingdoms, plantae and animalia. But along came the microscope, and there was another problem. All living things weren't just plants and animals. With the invention of the microscope, we learned about **protists** and **monerans**. In 1969, a fifth kingdom, **fungi**, was added when scientists discovered fungi cells are different from plant cells. Plant cells can make their own food by a process called **photosynthesis**. Fungi cells lack chlorophyll and are unable to carry out photosynthesis. Organisms that have similar traits or characteristics, such as cell structure, cell specialization, and a method of obtaining food are grouped together in the same kingdoms. The five-kingdom system is still commonly used by scientists today.

The Kingdoms

Monera: include microscopic organisms that are one-celled prokaryotes (do not have membrane-bound organelles or parts). All bacteria belong to this group.

Protista: include unicellular and multicellular eukaryotes (have organelles surrounded by membranes). Amoebas, algae, and kelp belong to this group.

Fungi: are mostly multicellular eukaryotes that have cell walls like plants but lack chlorophyll, so they cannot make their own food. They absorb their nutrients from a food source. Molds and mildews, mushrooms, and yeast make up this kingdom.

Classification

Plantae: are multicellular eukaryotes with specialized cells that form tissues, which are organized to form organs. Flowering plants, cone-bearing plants, ferns, and mosses belong to this kingdom.

Animalia: are multicellular eukaryotes with specialized cells that form tissues and organs. These organisms can move about to obtain food. Sponges, jellyfish, worms, sea stars, fish, frogs, turkeys, snakes, and people all belong to this kingdom.

Levels of Classification

Linnaeus's system divided each of the kingdoms into levels. The levels form a hierarchy from the broadest, most general group, all the way down to the smallest and most specific group. At each level, the organisms that share the most characteristics are grouped together.

Naming Organisms

What do crawdads, crayfish, and a mudbug have in common? Everything, because these are all common names for the same species. Clear communication among scientists throughout the world required an international system for naming organisms. Linnaeus developed a two-word naming system called **binomial nomenclature**. It was based on the Latin language because all scientists used Latin at that time. Because Latin was no longer a spoken language, the meanings of the words were not likely to change. Meanings of words do change in spoken languages. For example, *bad* used to mean something negative, but today some people say *bad* to mean something positive or good. *Cool* used to refer to temperature, but today *cool* can also mean "excellent." How many common names can you think of for the word *money*?

Kingdom
Animalia

Phylum or division
Chordata

Class
Amphibia

Order
Anura

Family
Hylidae

Genus
Hyla

Species
regilla

The international two-word naming system gives every organism its scientific name. Every organism has a scientific name to avoid confusion in communication. The genus name and the species name used together give the organism its scientific name. The genus name is first and is always capitalized, while the species name is second and is not capitalized. Both words are always printed in italics or underlined.

© Mark Twain Media, Inc., Publishers   13

Name: _____ Date: _____

Classification: *Reinforcement Activity*

To the student observer: Do you have something you have classified to make it easier for yourself?

_____

Analyze: Why is it important for all organisms to have a scientific name?

_____

_____

_____

1. What is taxonomy? _____

    _____

2. Why didn't Aristotle's system work? _____

    _____

    _____

    _____

3. Why do scientists group organisms? _____

    _____

    _____

4. What are the five kingdoms? _____

    _____

    _____

5. Why are the levels of classification often represented in an upside down triangle?

    _____

    _____

    _____

6. What is the scientific name for the Pacific tree frog? _____

    _____

7. What do we call the two-part naming system we still use today? _____

    _____

© Mark Twain Media, Inc., Publishers

Classification of Amphibians: *Amphibian Orders*

Kingdom: *Animalia*
    Phylum: *Chordata*
        Subphylum: *Vertebrata*
            Class: *Amphibia*
                Means "double life"

    Amphibians, like all living things, are **classified** (placed into groups), which makes it easier to learn about them. Classification is based on common ancestors in the same way you are related to your family members.

    Scientists have identified over 4,000 species of amphibians. It is difficult to keep track of so many amphibians. To ease their burden, taxonomists have divided all the known amphibians into one of three groups. Taxonomists do not group organisms simply because they look alike. They study their cells, the way they grow and develop, their blood, and even their internal and external body structures before deciding in which group they belong.

Amphibian Groups

    Amphibians have been divided into one of these three **orders** (groups) according to their body structures.

1. **Anura:** The largest group; frogs and toads—the tailless amphibians
2. **Urodela:** The newts and salamanders—the amphibians with tails
3. **Apoda:** The smallest group; caecilians—the wormlike (legless) amphibians

The Three Orders for Class Amphibia

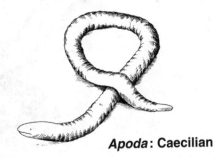

Apoda : **Caecilian**

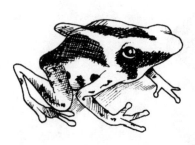

Anura : **Frog**

Urodela : **Salamander**

© Mark Twain Media, Inc., Publishers

Classification of Amphibians: *Amphibian Orders (cont.)*

Caecilians—"Little-Known Amphibians"

Class: *Amphibia*
  Order: *Apoda*

    Caecilians are very peculiar amphibians; they are not like the others. Many people have been fooled by this organism. They are long-bodied, without limbs, and almost tailless. If you saw one, you would probably think it was a worm. Caecilians even have scales that ring the body, giving it the segmented-worm look. Unlike worms, caecilians have the internal skeleton of a vertebrate. There are only 163 species of caecilians, making them the smallest order. A few species are **aquatic** (live in water), but most are **terrestrial** (live on land). They live in the tropics and are very common in parts of Africa, Asia, and Central and South America.

    Caecilians are the "little-known" amphibians because humans rarely see them. They are adapted to a life of burrowing in the soil. They use their hard, solid skulls to burrow and dig for food. They have tiny eyes and cannot see well, but they have an excellent sense of smell, which helps them catch their food. They eat worms and insects that live in the soil.

    Caecilians reproduce by internal fertilization, which is another reason they are not like the other amphibians. In some species the female lays eggs, and she guards them until they hatch. In other species, the females produce live young.

Classification of Amphibians: *Amphibian Orders (cont.)*

Salamanders and Newts—"Amphibians With Tails"

Class: *Amphibia*
   Order: *Urodela*

Salamanders, newts, and their relatives make up the amphibian order *Urodela*. Salamanders have long bodies, long tails, and two pairs of legs. Most live in the temperate climates of North America, Asia, and Europe; some live in the tropics of Central and South America. Salamanders are often mistaken for lizards.

Salamanders have a wide variety of habitats. Some live entirely on land, some live entirely in water, and some live in both water and on land. Those that live on land still need a moist habitat in order to survive. The skin of a salamander lets water pass right through it. If it is exposed to dry conditions, it will lose too much water and die. What would be a good damp place on land for a salamander?

Most salamanders breathe with lungs, but a large part of their oxygen is absorbed through their moist skin. The largest family of salamanders doesn't have lungs at all. These salamanders breathe only through their mouth and skin. In a salamander's skin are many glands. Some of these glands produce a **toxin** (poison). Poisonous salamanders are usually brightly-colored to warn predators to leave them alone.

The larvae of most salamanders live in rivers, lakes, streams, or ponds. Aquatic larvae have gills for respiration. In most adult salamanders, lungs replace the gills. Some urodelans live entirely in water, so they retain their gills as adults.

Mudpuppies

The group of salamanders called mudpuppies does not go through all the stages of metamorphosis. Mudpuppies have very small limbs that are useless on land, and they retain their larval form throughout their lives. The newt is another aquatic salamander, but it does not retain its gills as an adult. It must surface or climb out of the water from time to time.

Mole Salamanders

As the name implies, mole salamanders live underground. The spotted salamander or tiger salamander may be seen during the springtime during breeding season.

Blind Salamanders and Brook Salamanders

Blind salamanders and brook salamanders have very limited ranges. They live in springs or caves. The blind salamanders live only in underground caves or springs and have adapted to total darkness. They have no skin pigmentation, and their eyes are nonfunctional. The skin is transparent, which means you can see through it and watch what is going on inside.

© Mark Twain Media, Inc., Publishers

17

Classification of Amphibians: *Amphibian Orders (cont.)*

Frogs and Toads—"Tailless Amphibians"

Class: *Amphibia*
   Order: *Anura*

Frogs and toads are the most abundant and easily recognized amphibians. They make up the largest order, *Anura*. There are approximately 3,500 species of frogs and toads, but new species are still being discovered every year. They are found on all the continents except Antarctica. They live in colder, high-altitude conditions or dry, arid deserts; however, the greatest variety live in the tropical rain forests.

Frogs and toads also have a wide range of habitats. Their lifestyles include: **aquatic** (live in water), **terrestrial** (live on land), and **arboreal** (live in trees). Frogs and toads come in many different sizes, shapes, and colors; this enables them to survive such **diverse** (varied) habitats.

Frog or Toad?

Separating frogs and toads is not an easy task. The general features used to describe them do not always apply. In general, frogs are more slender, more active (faster), found in or near water, and have smooth skin, long hind legs, and fully-webbed feet. Toads tend to be less active (slower), prefer land, and have dry, bumpy skin, shorter legs, and little webbing of feet. However, some frogs do not live near water and have little or no webbing of their feet, while some toads have smooth, moist skin.

Hind view of a frog
Smooth skin and long hind legs

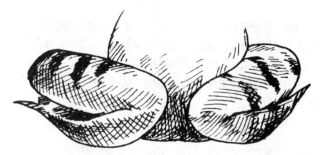

Hind view of a toad
Dry, bumpy skin and short hind legs

© Mark Twain Media, Inc., Publishers

Name: _____ Date: _____

Classification of Amphibians: *Reinforcement Activity*

To the student observer: Do you know what classification is based on? _____

_____

Analyze: Why do you feel taxonomy is such a difficult task and an ongoing challenge?

_____

_____

_____

Directions: Answer the following questions using what you have learned from the Classification of Amphibians lesson.

1. How did taxonomists ease the burden of keeping track of so many amphibians?

   _____

   _____

2. What do taxonomists study before they decide into which group an amphibian belongs?

   _____

   _____

   _____

3. What are the three orders of amphibians? _____

   _____

4. Which order is known as the little-known amphibians? Why? _____

   _____

   _____

5. In which order do the amphibians with tails belong? _____

6. Why is a salamander often mistaken for a lizard? _____

   _____

   _____

7. What is the largest order of amphibians? _____

8. What are the three habitats of frogs and toads? _____

   _____

   _____

© Mark Twain Media, Inc., Publishers

Order Anura: *Frogs and Toads*

Scientists have divided frogs and toads into 17 different families. They used several traits to help them accomplish this task. Study the traits below and read about some of these amphibian families. See if you can identify the frogs and toads on page 22 according to their family traits.

The following traits were used to divide the Anura into their family groups.

Foot shape	Number of warts	Pupil shape
Smoothness of skin	Coloration and patterns	Cranial ridges
Reproductive habits	Call or shape of vocal sacs	Coloration and patterns
Arrangement of parotoid glands		

A Few Happy Families of Frogs and Toads

Pelobatidae

The spadefoot toads, family *Pelobatidae*, have vertical pupils, no parotoid glands, live in arid regions, and need water and temporary pools to breed in. They estivate or burrow to avoid hot, dry conditions for up to three years. When rains make suitable conditions, they return. The pools dry up fast, so metamorphosis from tadpole to adult form takes place quickly—two to six weeks in most species. These toads secrete a very toxic poison.

Microhylidae

The narrow-mouthed frogs, family *Microhylidae*, are shy frogs that can be found on dark, damp nights near anthills. They are plump, medium-sized frogs with pointed heads that have a fold of skin across the back side of the head, and they appear to run rather than hop when frightened.

Bufonidae

Bufonidae is the most familiar and numerous family, the true toads. They have dry, warty skin, parotoid glands, and are very vocal, with inflatable throat pouches called **vocal sacs**. Different species have their own unique calls, which help to identify them. A typical bufonid has a compact body and short legs. It produces a toxic secretion, so it is necessary to wash your hands after handling one. Bufonids can eat huge quantities of insects.

Discoglossidae

Discoglossidae are characterized by a disc-shaped tongue, which is entirely fastened to the floor of the mouth. They cannot flip their tongues out to catch prey like other frogs. They have strong forelimbs, and some of the males carry the eggs around on their hind legs until the tadpoles are ready to hatch.

Pipidae

There are 26 species of the aquatic family *Pipidae*. All have powerful hind legs with huge, heavily-webbed hind feet, and they have small forelimbs. Their eyes and nostrils are positioned on the tops of their heads; they are unique in the fact that they do not have tongues at all. Some species have flattened bodies. The pipidae eggs are embedded on the back of the female.

Order Anura: *Frogs and Toads (cont.)*

Ascaphidae

There is only one species in the family *Ascaphidae*. The main trait is its taillike structure. Ascaphidae do not have true tails but have tail-wagging muscles that give the appearance of a tail. The tailed frog lives in North America in mountain streams and damp forests.

Leptodactylidae

Leptodactylidae is a large, diverse family of tropical frogs. A few have managed to range into the southwestern United States. Their anatomy is very similar to the tree frogs in that they have disc-shaped suckers on the end of each digit. However, these frogs differ in their reproductive habits. They usually lay their eggs on land near running water, and the metamorphosis or change takes place inside the egg. The males have a high, whistling call. The white-lipped frog builds a nest that looks like egg whites out of glandular secretions and then lays its eggs in the nest. The young larvae live in the nest until rains provide them an opportunity to swim to a nearby pond.

Hylidae

The tree frogs belong to the large family *Hylidae*. There are over 600 species living over most of the warmer parts of the world except in Africa and southern Asia. Family Hylidae includes tree frogs, cricket frogs, and chorus frogs. Tree frogs have long legs and a rather flattened, small body, which helps them balance and snuggle up close to the tree trunk or leaves when they are resting. They have large areas of sticky webbing between their toes. They have extra bones that help them curl their toes around thin twigs. These adaptations make them very good climbers. The eyes of tree frogs are very large and face forward. Tree frogs are **nocturnal** (active at night) because many insects are also active at night. Cricket frogs are non-climbing and live on the ground or under ground. Members of this family can be a variety of beautiful colors, and they are very noisy singers. Some females in this family have egg pouches on their backs. The tadpoles develop while riding around in the pouch and emerge as froglets after being protected during that vulnerable part of their lives.

Ranidae

Ranidae are the true frogs; this family includes the familiar pond frogs. This large, successful family totals 667 species, which are good at jumping and swimming. They have smooth, moist skin; the males have paired or single vocal sacs on their throats. They are found on all the continents except Antarctica. Most live near fresh water; however, a few species can thrive in **brackish** (slightly salty) water. This family produces the frog legs that many humans find tasty.

Rhinodermatidae

The mouth-brooding frogs belong to the South American family *Rhinodermatidae*. These frogs are small with pointed snouts. There are only two species in this small family. They are very similar to the Leptodactylidae family. The male frogs in this group have a strange reproductive habit. After the females lay a small cluster of terrestrial eggs, the male watches closely until it sees the tadpoles begin to move inside the jelly. It then picks them up with its mouth and holds them inside its vocal sac until the tadpoles are fully developed. Then it spits them out.

© Mark Twain Media, Inc., Publishers

Name: _____ Date: _____

Order Anura: *Which Frog or Toad Are You?*

To the student observer: Identify the proper family for each of the frogs and toads listed in the word bank below.

A. _____

B. _____

C. _____

D. _____

E. _____

F. _____

G. _____

H. _____

I. _____

J. _____

ANURA FAMILIES WORD BANK

Leptodactylidae	Pelobatidae
Pipidae	Microhylidae
Discoglossidae	Bufonidae
Ascaphidae	Hylidae
Rhinodermatidae	Ranidae

© Mark Twain Media, Inc., Publishers

Amphibian Behavior

Behavior is the way an organism acts. Most animal behavior is based on survival. The behavior is usually a response to something in the environment. Animals have unique, instinctive behavioral adaptations that help them survive in their surroundings.

Where Amphibians Live

Most amphibians live in or near water, and water plays a vital role in their behavior. Amphibians need fresh water to keep their skin moist and to reproduce, but they rarely drink water as we do. Water passes quickly through their skin. To reduce water loss, they seek damp, shady places and burrow into underground chambers. They usually stay hidden during the day and come out at night in search of food.

How Amphibians Protect Themselves

Amphibians have many enemies. Most of their enemies are animals that eat them. Although most amphibians produce a poisonous chemical in their skin, they cannot inflict it on their enemies as snakes or spiders can. Some amphibians secrete a poisonous substance produced by the **parotoid gland**. The parotoid is located behind the eyes and near the ears or tympanic membrane. Poisonous amphibians usually have bright colors to warn their enemies, so they can defend their territories. They have numerous methods of displaying these colors.

Amphibians also play hide-and-seek to protect themselves. They are masters of camouflage. Their colorations help them to blend in with their surroundings. They also have skin flaps and fringes that help them disguise their body outlines to look like natural objects in the environment. Some have a line down their backs that breaks up their body shapes and helps hide them from predators. If their color is a good match to their surroundings and they remain still, it is almost impossible to see them.

Amphibians also demonstrate startling behaviors that surprise predators. They bluff enemies by puffing up to increase their size or arching their backs to show warning coloration. They may jump and face the danger head-on or simply jump away. Some salamanders wave their tail in the air. When a predator grabs it, the tail breaks off, and the salamander escapes. A new tail grows to replace the old one. Some amphibians may open their mouths and scream an alarm, curl up their tails, play dead, or become prickly by pushing out needle-like rib tips through their sides. Another species surprises its enemies by exposing eyespots on its backside. Now that behavior is bound to cause confusion! The behaviors, such as jumping away; breaking tails; hiding or dazzling with color; secreting a poison; or camouflage and bluffing, give the amphibian a chance to escape.

Amphibian Behavior (cont.)

Senses for Survival

Like all animals, amphibians have five basic senses—touch, taste, sight, smell, and hearing. They also can detect ultraviolet light and the earth's magnetic field. They feel temperature changes and know when it is time to estivate or hibernate. They feel pain and respond to irritants such as acids in the environment. They must respond quickly to external changes. In terrestrial species, a sudden temperature change can lead to death by causing them to lose too much moisture. They use their senses to hunt for food. They like "fast food." They only eat living things that move, and they snatch it up fast. They also rely on their senses of hearing and sight to attract a mate and to avoid enemies. Some aquatic amphibians have a lateral line sensory system for detecting pressure changes that help them avoid objects in water. Most amphibians have good vision, especially night vision.

Ecological Roles

Amphibians are important to humans. After all, they are a good food source. Many people enjoy eating frog legs. Amphibians also help to control insect populations that could destroy crops and transmit diseases. Some scientists are watching amphibians closely. Because of their porous skin and unshelled eggs, they are very vulnerable to changes in the environment. They are good biological indicators. A **bioindicator** is an organism whose health serves as an indicator of the health of the ecosystem. In recent years, researchers have noticed a rapid drop in the amphibian population worldwide and are trying to find out what has caused it. Some hypothesize that it is due to an increase in solar radia-

A mutated salamander with five legs is shown above. Researchers believe that air and water pollution are endangering the amphibian population.

tion. Others believe that air and water pollution or global warming may be the cause. Hopefully, researchers will find the cause before it is too late for the populations of amphibians to recover. If the cause is not found and corrected, other populations may begin to decline in the future as well.

Name: _____ Date: _____

Amphibian Behavior: *Reinforcement Activity*

To the student observer: Can you give an example of amphibian behavior and tell what caused the behavior?

_____

_____

Analyze: Why is it important to know what is causing the rapid decline of some amphibians?

_____

_____

Directions: Complete the following statements.

1. _____ is the way an organism acts.

2. Amphibians have many _____.

3. Amphibians prevent water loss by seeking _____ places and burrowing into

   _____ _____.

4. The parotoid gland produces a _____ in the amphibian's skin.

5. Poisonous amphibians have _____ colors to warn their enemies.

6. Amphibians come out at _____ to find food.

Directions: Answer the questions below about amphibian behavior.

7. List three ways amphibians protect themselves. _____

   _____

   _____

   _____

8. Why are amphibians considered masters of camouflage? _____

   _____

   _____

9. What are the five basic senses all animals have? _____

   _____

10. What is a bioindicator? _____

   _____

Metamorphosis: *How Frogs Develop*

Observers, have you ever been near a pond on a summer evening? If so, you have probably heard a loud, deep noise; that noise was the croaking of frogs. The bullfrogs are our largest frogs and have very loud voices. If you were observant, you probably noticed a bright yellow throat on some of the frogs. This tells you that this is a male bullfrog. Female bullfrogs do not have bright yellow throats. It is the males who do most of the singing. When the frogs are young, they do not look like they do when they are full-grown.

At night during the springtime, a female frog will lay its eggs in the pond where she lives. She will lay a great many eggs called **frogspawn**. They will look like little black and white balls covered with a clear jelly. The jelly holds them all together in a huge mass. (Remember, frog eggs do not have shells.) The egg mass is shaped like a pancake and clings to sticks near the edge of the pond. The eggs are not fertile when the female lays them. The male frog embraces the female and begins fertilizing the eggs in the water as she lays them. This is called **external fertilization** (fertilization outside the female's body).

The frogs have not had anything to eat since they woke up from their winter nap called **hibernation**. After mating, they leave the eggs and go in search of food. Frogs do not provide care for their young. The eggs begin to grow at once. Each little ball begins to resemble a bean. In about a week, the eggs are ready to hatch. A young frog is a **tadpole** (or polliwog) that can't do much except hold on to the jelly it hatched from. Soon tiny fringes grow on each side of its head. These fringes are its gills for breathing. When it is about a day old, it begins to swim by moving its tail. On the second or third day, it develops eyes and a mouth. It then begins to nibble on plants. This begins the larva stage during metamorphosis. The tadpole is very lucky if it lives this long. Other animals that live in the pond eat most of the tadpoles.

The tadpole begins to change. Folds of skin grow over the gills for protection. To breathe, the tadpole gulps the water into its mouth. The water passes over the gills, which takes the oxygen from the water. Air (oxygen) is dissolved in the water. After the water passes over the gills, it goes out a little hole on the left side of its body. This hole is called a **breathing hole**.

A tadpole spends the entire summer eating, growing, and trying to escape from enemies that might eat it. By fall, the tadpole is about one and one-half inches long. As the weather begins to get chilly, the tadpole swims to the bottom of the pond where it burrows into the mud and falls asleep. The tadpole hibernates for the winter months. In the spring, it wakes up and is soon busily eating little plants as fast as it can. By midsummer, the tadpole will be about 5 inches long. Then, at the base of its tail, little hind legs begin to form. In a few weeks, these legs are long and strong. Soon the front legs begin forming inside the tadpole's body. The legs push their way out, and the tadpole now has four legs. At this point, it is nearly an adult frog. As breathing becomes more difficult, it begins to take in gulps of air, and its lungs quickly begin to grow. Its mouth is getting bigger, and a big sticky tongue has grown inside. While its mouth is changing, it cannot eat. It must live off its tail. The tadpole gradually absorbs its tail into its body. The tadpole is now beginning to look like an adult frog. Its eyes begin to bulge, and it practices breathing with its nose. Now it is ready to climb up out of the water.

The change during the development of the young frog is called **metamorphosis** (change of body form and appearance). Amphibians and insects go through changes during their life cycles. During its life cycle, an amphibian changes the way it looks. The change from newly-hatched tadpole to fully-formed frog takes about 12–16 weeks, but this span of time is greatly

© Mark Twain Media, Inc., Publishers

Metamorphosis: *How Frogs Develop (cont.)*

affected by the species, water temperature, and food supply. Bullfrogs take the longest; they may not go through metamorphosis for over a year or more. Tadpoles found in colder regions or high altitudes may have to winter in the tadpole stage and not turn into a frog until the following spring. Not all frogs and toads have free-living tadpoles. For some, development takes place within an egg or the body of a parent.

Frog Metamorphosis

Stage one: Egg stage

    a. Fertilized egg mass

    b. Embryo develops—hatches in six days

Stage two: Larva stage; tadpole or polliwog stage

    c. Just hatched—poorly developed; feeds on yolk; attaches to weeds; feeds and swims at 7–10 days

    d. Frills (external gills) disappear and internal gills form—4 weeks; becomes active

    e. Hind legs bud—6–9 weeks; half-tadpole and half-frog

    f. Young frog stage—10–12 weeks; four legs; tail begins to be absorbed

Stage three: Adult stage

    g. Adult frog—16 weeks

Egg mass

Adult Frog

Young Frog

Tadpole

Larva

Name: _____ Date: _____

Metamorphosis: *Reinforcement Activity*

To the student observer: What happened to the tadpole's tail? _____
_____

Analyze: Why do you think frogs lay so many eggs at one time? _____
_____

Directions: Answer the following questions about metamorphosis.

1. What is metamorphosis? _____
    _____

2. What two classes of animals go through metamorphosis? _____
    _____

3. What are the three stages of metamorphosis? _____
    _____
    _____

4. How can you tell if a bullfrog is a male or female? _____
    _____

5. When do female frogs lay their eggs? _____

6. What is the egg mass called? _____

7. Do frogs take care of their offspring? _____

8. How many weeks does it take for tadpoles to develop into frogs? _____
    _____

9. What affects the amount of time spent in the larva stage? _____
    _____
    _____

10. What is the advantage of the jellylike coating around the eggs? _____
    _____
    _____

11. On your own paper, model metamorphosis by developing a flow chart that shows the stages of frog development.

Name: _____ Date: _____

Grow Up, Tadpoles!: *Observation Activity*

Materials you will need for observation:

Small bucket
Pond water, stones, underwater plants
Stick or large rock
Gravel
A small piece of meat on a string
An aquarium tank with lid
Hand lens

Procedure:

1. Have an adult or your teacher help you find some frogspawn in a nearby stream or pond. In a small bucket, collect plants, stones, and water. (Perhaps your teacher can bring some to class.)
2. Next, prepare your tank by covering the bottom with clean gravel. (Obtain gravel from a pet store.) Fill the tank with pond water. Anchor the plants with stones. Put the stick or large rock in the tank for the young frogs to climb onto above the water level. Place the tank in a place where it will receive filtered sunlight. Let the water settle for two or three days.
3. Transfer the spawn into the tank (very carefully). Watch the spawn every day. Within three weeks, tadpoles should hatch.
4. After the hind legs appear, place a small piece of meat in the tank (attached to a string).
5. Observe the tadpoles for about three months. Record data on your observation sheet.
6. When the young frogs begin to climb out of the water onto the stick or rock, take them back to the pond or stream where they came from and turn them loose.

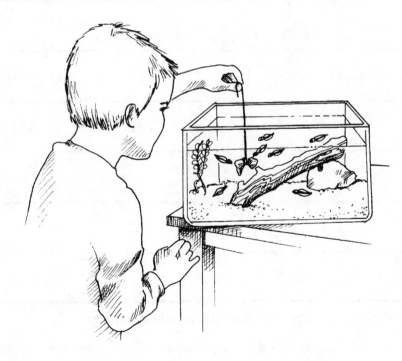

© Mark Twain Media, Inc., Publishers

Name: _____ Date: _____

Grow Up, Tadpoles!: *Observation Activity (cont.)*

	Data Table
Week	**Observations**
1	
2	
3	
4	
5	
6	
7	
8	
9	
10	
11	
12	
13	
14	

On the following page, answer the questions and conclusions.

© Mark Twain Media, Inc., Publishers   30

Name: _____ Date: _____

Grow Up, Tadpoles!: *Questions and Conclusions*

1. How many weeks did it take for the tadpoles to hatch? _____

2. Did the tadpoles swim alone or in a group? _____

    _____

    _____

3. How do tadpoles obtain oxygen? How do you know? _____

    _____

    _____

    _____

    _____

4. Describe how the tadpoles obtained their food. _____

    _____

    _____

    _____

    _____

5. Which legs appeared first, the front or back? _____

    _____

6. How long did it take for the frogs to have all four legs? _____

    _____

7. When did the young frogs start climbing onto the rock or stick? What does this indicate?

    _____

    _____

    _____

    _____

8. Did you notice that the young frogs lost their tadpole tails? When did this happen, and
    where did the tail go?

    _____

    _____

    _____

    _____

Name: _____ Date: _____

The Color of Frogs: *Amphibian Observation Activity*

Observers, the amphibian is a fascinating vertebrate to study. Amphibians have an amazing ability to adapt to many environments. Many amphibians have the ability to change color. They change color to camouflage themselves from enemies and to control their body temperatures. Let's explore how a common grass frog changes its color.

Problem: Can frogs really change their colors as needed?

Materials:
2 terrariums—an aquarium that has a complete environment to support both plant and animal life is called a **terrarium**.
2 grass frogs
soil
land plants
window screening or mesh lid
rocks
some water

Procedure:
1. Set up 2 terrariums with soil, land plants, rocks at one end, and water at the other end.
2. Place a frog in each terrarium. Cover each tank with screening to prevent them from jumping out.
3. Note the color of each frog in your notebook or science journal. Place each of the terrariums in a different environment. Place one tank where it will receive light. Put the other terrarium in a dark place such as a cabinet or closet. Leave them both undisturbed for 15 minutes. Make a prediction as to what kind of results you expect to receive from this observation.
4. After 15 minutes, note the color of the frogs again in your notebooks or journals.
5. Compare your prediction to the actual results.

Questions and conclusions:

1. Did the color of the frogs change? _____ What was the color of the frog that was

   placed in the dark? _____

2. Did your results allow you to accept or reject your hypothesis (prediction)?

   _____

   _____

3. Is it beneficial to a frog to change its skin color? Explain your answer. _____

   _____

   _____

Keeping an Eye to the Future: *Disappearance of the Cascades Frogs*

Observers, we must realize how important species diversity is to an ecosystem. Each species has a job or role to fulfill. If something happens to just one part of the ecosystem, it directly or indirectly has an effect on other parts. If a species begins to struggle to survive in its ecosystem, there is usually a reason.

Amphibians are on the decline at a rapid rate. Because they live on land and in water, they are affected by chemical changes that take place in both areas. Some of the decline is due to loss of habitat by clear-cutting forests, acid rain, and pesticides. The introduction of game fish (new enemies) and the depletion of the ozone need to be added to the list of possible causes for the decline.

Cascades Frogs and Ultraviolet Light

The Cascades frog lives in a remote area of the Cascade Mountains of California, Oregon, and Washington. There doesn't seem to be evidence of pollution in this remote mountainous region, yet the eggs of this frog are dying, and scientists think they know why. The eggs are laid in clear, shallow water and are exposed to a great deal of sunlight. As the ozone layer becomes thinner, more ultraviolet rays are getting through. It appears that the ultraviolet light is damaging the eggs' DNA (hereditary code). Scientists have been studying the eggs and have tested different levels of exposure and have found that the results support their hypothesis. They began to wonder why other amphibian eggs were not affected. They compared the eggs of the Cascades frog to the eggs of the Pacific tree frog, which is not suffering from a decline. In that study, they found the Pacific tree frog eggs were producing three times the amount of **photolyase** (an enzyme) as the eggs of the Cascades frogs, making them less likely to die as a result of ultraviolet light.

People must be aware of how their actions affect the environment and the wildlife that lives there. Like all animals, amphibians have their roles to fulfill and have the right to live undisturbed in their natural habitats. People have caused many problems for amphibians. We are cutting down the rain forests, filling in natural ponds, and contributing to the pollution of air and water. Amphibians already have many enemies; humans do not need to contribute to their struggle.

© Mark Twain Media, Inc., Publishers

Name: _____ Date: _____

Keeping an Eye to the Future: *Conservation Reinforcement*

To the student observer: Explore the concepts below. Based on what you have learned from this lesson, write a brief paragraph stating and supporting your point of view.

Explore the Concept: If ultraviolet light damages the DNA (hereditary code) of frog eggs, do you think it could also damage the DNA of other organisms?

_____

_____

_____

_____

_____

_____

_____

_____

_____

Brainstorm: If you were one of these researchers, what would you do to try and reduce harm from ultraviolet light exposure?

_____

_____

_____

_____

_____

_____

_____

_____

_____

_____

© Mark Twain Media, Inc., Publishers

Name: _____ Date: _____

Where Did All the Frogs Go?: *Creative Writing Assignment*

To the student observer: Issues are more easily understood if they become part of a fictional story. Using the information you have learned in this unit on amphibians and conservation, write a story involving a frog faced with a problem in its environment. Think about your story before you begin. On your own paper, make a web of story ideas and issues to help you. Write your story and illustrate it in some way.

Think before you write:

1. Select an amphibian.

2. Determine the problem your amphibian is going to face in its environment.

3. Apply the 5 W's and How:

    Who is it about?

    What is the major problem facing your main character?

    When did this happen?

    Where does the story take place?

    Why did the problem occur?

    How is the problem going to be resolved? (If it can be resolved?)

* **Teacher Note:** It will take some time to create a finished story. Don't expect to finish this in one class period. If you have a computer lab, you could let students create their stories on the computer. Cooperative learning could be used for this assignment as well.

Name: _____ Date: _____

Can Endangered Amphibians Recover?: *Conservation/ Research*

To the student observer: Humans have had a significant role in the population decline of many animals. People are now getting deeply concerned that their natural heritage be preserved for future generations. Research what is being done to help wildlife survive and thrive on our planet. Research threatened and endangered amphibians to learn what is being done to help them recover. After you have researched this topic, answer the questions below.

1. What are some things being done to help threatened and endangered animals?

   _____

   _____

   _____

   _____

   _____

2. List some endangered amphibians that have begun to recover, and explain what was done to help them.

   _____

   _____

   _____

   _____

   _____

3. List two things you and your family could do to help amphibians or any other animals have a safe future.

   _____

   _____

   _____

   _____

   _____

* **Teacher Note:** This makes an excellent cooperative learning Internet activity. Have resource materials available as well. Guide students through the frustration of doing research.

© Mark Twain Media, Inc., Publishers

Amphibian Vocabulary: *Study Sheet*

To the student observer: Below is a list of important terms for the amphibian unit. Use this list of terms and their definitions to help you complete the activities on the following pages. This study sheet will also help you prepare for the unit test.

1. **Adult** - the final stage of the life cycle

2. **Amphibian** - a cold-blooded vertebrate without scales

3. **Aquatic** - refers to animals who live in water

4. **Arboreal** - refers to animals who live in trees

5. **Camouflage** - protective coloration that helps organisms hide

6. **Endoskeleton** - an internal skeleton

7. **Estivation** - a dormant state to avoid hot, dry conditions

8. **Gills** - a respiratory organ in aquatic animals

9. **Herpetology** - the study of amphibians and reptiles

10. **Hibernation** - a dormant state to avoid cold conditions

11. **Larva** - immature stage in metamorphosis; tadpole stage

12. **Metamorphosis** - the process of change in form from larva to adult

13. **Parotoid gland** - produces a toxin in the skin of some amphibians

14. **Predator** - animal who hunts and eats other animals

15. **Respiration** - the process of exchanging oxygen and carbon dioxide

16. **Skeleton** - a framework that shapes and supports the body

17. **Spinal cord** - a thick bundle of nerves that runs through the backbone

18. **Terrestrial** - refers to animals who live on land

19. **Toxic** - poisonous

20. **Vertebrate** - an animal with a backbone

© Mark Twain Media, Inc., Publishers

Name: _____   Date: _____

Amphibians: *Crossword Puzzle*

To the student observer: Use what you have learned about amphibians to complete the cross-word puzzle below.

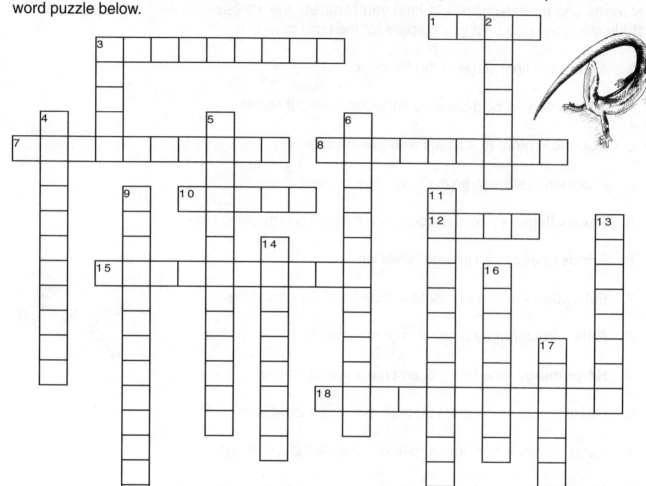

ACROSS

1. A tailless amphibian
3. Means "double life"
7. An animal with a backbone
8. Amphibian populations are _____ rapidly.
10. Poisonous
12. An amphibian with a tail
15. The wormlike amphibians
18. The study of amphibians and reptiles
19. Protective coloration

DOWN

2. Describes an animal that lives in water
3. Final stage in metamorphosis
4. Describes an animal that lives on land
5. Produces a toxin (two words)
6. Composed of the spinal cord, nerves, and brain (two words)
9. The change in form from larva to adult
11. An internal skeleton
13. To put into groups
14. Frogs do this in the winter.
16. The science of classification
17. Phylum of amphibians

© Mark Twain Media, Inc., Publishers   38

Name: _____   Date: _____

Reviewing Key Concepts: *Amphibian Jeopardy*

Key Concepts:
- Amphibians are cold-blooded vertebrates with moist skin and no scales.
- Amphibians live part of their lives in water and part of their lives on land.
- Amphibians depend on water to reproduce.
- Amphibians lay eggs without shells.
- Amphibians have a life cycle and undergo a process called metamorphosis.
- There are three groups of amphibians.

To the student observer: You may be familiar with a popular game show in which the answers are given and the contestants must try to provide the right questions. See if you can correctly complete the questions for each of the following answers.

1. **Answer:** An animal that has a backbone

   Question: What is a (an) _____?

2. **Answer:** An internal skeleton

   Question: What is a (an) _____?

3. **Answer:** A process of shedding the exoskeleton in order to grow

   Question: What is _____?

4. **Answer:** Food, oxygen, and shelter

   Question: What are _____?

5. **Answer:** A framework that shapes and supports the body

   Question: What is a (an) _____?

6. **Answer:** The thick bundle of nerves that carries information to and from the brain

   Question: What is a (an) _____?

7. **Answer:** Cold-blooded vertebrates that live part of their lives in water and part of their lives on land

   Question: What are _____?

8. **Answer:** Most amphibians do not live to reach adulthood

   Question: Why do _____?

9. **Answer:** The science of classification

   Question: What is _____?

10. **Answer:** A scientist who studies amphibians and reptiles

    Question: What is a (an) _____?

11. **Answer:** A resting state to survive during the cold winter months

    Question: What is _____?

12. **Answer:** Cold-blooded animals that obtain body heat from outside sources

    Question: What are _____?

Name: _____ Date: _____

Reviewing Key Concepts: *Amphibian Jeopardy (cont.)*

13. **Answer:** A change in development as a young amphibian grows into an adult

    Question: What is _____?

14. **Answer:** The ancestors of amphibians

    Question: What are _____?

15. **Answer:** A two-word naming system that gives every organism a scientific name

    Question: What is _____?

16. **Answer:** The largest order of amphibians; it includes the tailless amphibians

    Question: What are _____?

17. **Answer:** Peculiar wormlike amphibians

    Question: What are _____?

18. **Answer:** An amphibian with a long body and a long tail

    Question: What is a (an) _____?

19. **Answer:** A less active amphibian that prefers land and has dry, bumpy skin

    Question: What is a (an) _____?

20. **Answer:** The way an organism acts

    Question: What is _____?

21. **Answer:** A gland in amphibians that produces a toxin

    Question: What are _____?

22. **Answer:** A protective coloration that blends in with the surroundings

    Question: What is _____?

23. **Answer:** An organism whose health indicates the health of the ecosystem

    Question: What is a (an) _____?

24. **Answer:** Egg, larva, and adult

    Question: What are _____?

25. **Answer:** The immature stage in amphibian development

    Question: What is a (an) _____?

26. **Answer:** The depletion of the ozone layer, clear cutting, acid rain, and pesticides

    Question: What are _____?

27. **Answer:** Ultraviolet light is damaging its eggs' DNA.

    Question: What is _____?

* **Teacher Note:** Use this activity to check students' understanding of amphibians as a reinforcement worksheet, as an evaluation, or as a fun game.

Name: _____ Date: _____

Amphibians: *Unit Test*

Multiple Choice

Directions: Write the letter of the correct answer on the line at the left.

_____ 1. The skull and the vertebrae are part of the _____.

    a. circulatory system   b. endoskeleton   c. exoskeleton   d. digestive system

_____ 2. The backbone of a vertebrate protects its _____.

    a. vertebrae   b. brain   c. exoskeleton   d. spinal cord

_____ 3. There are _____ main groups of amphibians.

    a. one   b. two   c. three   d. four

_____ 4. A young frog is sometimes called a _____.

    a. newt   b. polliwog   c. chameleon   d. lamprey

_____ 5. The main characteristic of all vertebrates is the presence of _____.

    a. cartilage   b. a large brain   c. a backbone   d. an exoskeleton

_____ 6. Amphibians need moisture in order to _____.

    a. breathe   b. catch prey   c. move   d. maintain their body temperature

_____ 7. Vertebrates belong to the phylum _____.

    a. Amphibia   b. Mammalia   c. Arthropoda   d. Chordata

_____ 8. Young amphibians take oxygen from water through their _____.

    a. lungs   b. air sacs   c. gills   d. swim bladders

_____ 9. _____ are ectothermic vertebrates with moist, scaleless skin that lay their eggs in water.

    a. fish   b. reptiles   c. lancelets   d. salamanders

_____ 10. _____ is a period of inactivity in the winter.

    a. estivation   b. hibernation   c. fertilization   d. gestation

Name: _____ Date: _____

Amphibians: *Unit Test (cont.)*

Matching

Directions: Place the letter of the definition on the right next to the correct term on the left.

_____	1. Parotoid Gland	A.	Worm-like amphibian
_____	2. Metamorphosis	B.	To put into groups
_____	3. Herpetology	C.	Science of classification
_____	4. Camouflage	D.	Living in trees
_____	5. Terrestrial	E.	Final stage of the life cycle of an amphibian
_____	6. Toxic	F.	Means "double life"
_____	7. Spinal cord	G.	The study of reptiles and amphibians
_____	8. Amphibian	H.	Living in water
_____	9. Caecilian	I.	Poisonous
_____	10. Taxonomy	J.	Living on land
_____	11. Arboreal	K.	Thick bundle of nerves
_____	12. Classify	L.	Produces a toxin
_____	13. Adult	M.	A change in form
_____	14. Larva	N.	Used to blend in
_____	15. Aquatic	O.	Second stage of the life cycle of an amphibian

Answer Keys

Invertebrates and Vertebrates: Reinforcement (p. 3)
Student observer: Yes, a vertebrate has an internal skeleton or backbone, while an invertebrate does not.
Analyze: The presence or absence of a backbone
1. Invertebrates and vertebrates
2. A vertebrate has a backbone and an invertebrate does not.
3. The vertebrates
4. The invertebrates
5. The vertebrates
6. A skeleton on the outside of the animal
7. A skeleton on the inside of the animal that protects soft body parts
8. A hard, waterproof substance that makes up the exoskeleton
9. Molt its exoskeleton
10. An animal must have food, oxygen, and shelter in order to survive.

An Internal Affair: Reinforcement (p. 5)
Student Observer: Answers will vary.
Analyze: Your feet would be numb. The messages from external stimuli would not be sent to the brain.
1. A backbone is a column of bones along the animal's back. It protects the spinal cord, the passageway of nerves.
2. The backbone consists of vertebrae, cartilage, and the spinal cord.
3. The spinal cord is a thick bundle of nerves that carries information to and from the brain.
4. Messages cannot get through to the brain.
5. The nervous system is made up of the brain, spinal cord, and nerves. It controls the body's activities.
6. The skeleton is a framework that shapes and supports the animal's body. The skeleton helps the body move and protects body organs.

What Is an Amphibian?: Reinforcement (p. 7)
Student observer: Answers will vary. Some teachers will use this as an introductory question.
Analyze: They mate and lay their eggs in water; the eggs do not have a shell; they have gills when they are young; and their skin is not waterproof.

1. Amphibian
Means
Phylum
Heat
Internal
Body
Inside
Amphibians
Need
Substance
2a. Frogs and toads; salamanders, sirens, and newts; and caecilians
  b. They are vertebrates; are cold-blooded; most have smooth, moist skin; they live part of their lives in water and part on land; they use gills, lungs, or skin to obtain oxygen; and they lay eggs and mate in water. (any four)

Herpetology: "Crawling Things" (p. 9)
Student observer: Herpetology is the branch of science that deals with amphibians and reptiles.
Analyze: They studied live specimens and dissections of specimens and realized that reptiles and amphibians were different internally and developmentally.
1. Scientists thought amphibians and reptiles were closely related.
2. Cold-blooded animals that obtain body heat from outside sources; animals whose body temperatures change with their surroundings
3. A warm-blooded animal that maintains a constant body temperature
4. A cold-blooded animal does not have to maintain a constant body temperature. They can go without food for longer periods of time.
5. Hibernation is a resting state to survive the cold. The animal slows down all of its body functions and lives off stored fat.
6. An animal estivates if its body temperature is too high. It finds a cool spot and slows down all of its body functions.
7. Metamorphosis is a change in development as a young amphibian grows into an adult.

Ancient Amphibians: Reinforcement (p. 11)
Student observer: Lobe-finned fish
Analyze: When conditions get too dry, frogs bury themselves. The rain signals them that favorable conditions have returned, and the frogs suddenly reappear.
1. lobe-finned fish
2. Devonian
3a. Food: easy food sources without competition
 b. No predators
4. They are smaller in size, and there is less variety of species.
5a. Lungs: for breathing air
 b. Legs: for mobility on land; hip and shoulder girdles
 c. Flexible necks
  Other answers: eyelids, ears to hear in the air
6. They need to keep their skins moist because they have no scales to prevent water loss. They lay shell-less eggs in water and breathe through gills when they are young.
7. They are legless and breathe with gills.

Classification: Reinforcement (p. 14)
Student observer: Answers will vary. Possible answers include closets, CDs, baseball cards, etc.
Analyze: To avoid errors in communication; there is often more than one common name for an organism.
1. The science of classification
2. It was too general and had too many exceptions. There wasn't a logical place for amphibians.
3. To make it easier to study and learn about organisms
4. Monera, protista, fungi, plantae, and animalia
5. Each time they divide, the group gets smaller.
6. *Hyla regilla*
7. Binomial nomenclature

Classification of Amphibians: Reinforcement (p. 19)
Student Observer: It is based on common ancestors.
Analyze: There are so many species, and new ones are still being found.
1. Amphibians were divided into three groups.

2. What the amphibian looks like; its cells; the way it grows and develops; its blood; and its internal and external body structures
3. Anura, Urodela, Apoda
4. Apoda (the Caecilians); Humans rarely see them because they burrow in the soil.
5. Urodela
6. Salamanders have long bodies, long tails, and two pairs of legs like lizards.
7. Anura
8. Aquatic (water), terrestrial (land), and arboreal (trees)

Order Anura: Which Frog or Toad Are You? (p. 22)
A. Microhylidae
B. Leptodactylidae
C. Pelobatidae
D. Ascaphidae
E. Discoglossidae
F. Pipidae
G. Bufonidae
H. Hylidae
I. Ranidae
J. Rhinodermatidae

Amphibian Behavior: Reinforcement (p. 25)
Student observer: Answers will vary.
Analyze: Eventually the cause may affect other animals that aren't so sensitive. It might even have an effect on us.
1. Behavior
2. enemies
3. damp, underground chambers
4. poison (toxin)
5. bright
6. night
7. Produce a poisonous substance; camouflage; startling behaviors, such as jumping away, breaking their tails, screaming, or exposing eyespots (any three)
8. They have so many colors and blend in with their surroundings. They also can change or disguise their body outlines.
9. Touch, taste, smell, sight, and hearing
10. An organism whose health serves as an indicator of the health of the ecosystem in which it lives

How Frogs Develop: Reinforcement (p. 28)
Student observer: It was absorbed into the body.
Analyze: Only a few survive to reach adulthood because most are eaten by other animals.
1. A change in body form in becoming an adult

2. Insects and amphibians
3. Egg, larva, and adult
4. Males have a bright yellow throat.
5. In the spring
6. Frogspawn
7. Not usually
8. About 12–16 weeks; it varies with the species. Bullfrogs can take over a year.
9. The species, water temperature, and food supply
10. It offers protection.
11.

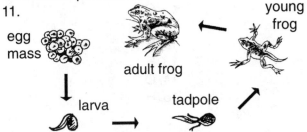

egg mass

adult frog

larva

tadpole

young frog

Grow Up, Tadpoles!: Questions and Conclusions (p. 31)

1. Within three weeks
2. Sometimes they swim in schools like fish; sometimes they swim alone.
3. They obtain oxygen from their gills. You could see the gills on the sides of the tadpoles.
4. They ate the plant material until they had hind legs.
5. The hind legs appeared first after eight weeks.
6. About 12 weeks
7. They began climbing when the gills disappeared. This indicated that they could obtain oxygen from the air because they had developed lungs.
8. Yes, they lost their tails after 13 or 14 weeks. The tails were absorbed into the bodies of the frogs as the young frogs grew.

The Color of Frogs: Amphibian Observation Activity (p. 32)

1. Yes, the color was dark to blend in with its surroundings. (The frog in the light should remain the same color.)
2. Answers will vary.
3. Yes, it helps them hide from predators.

Can Endangered Amphibians Recover?: Conservation/Research (p. 36)

1. Possible answers: (1) Government agencies have passed laws to ban or regulate the sale of animals and animal products and to restrict hunting. (2) Game refuges and parks have been set aside with strict use of the land enforced by rangers. (3) Pollution regulations are set by government agencies. (4) Education efforts are raising awareness. (5) Captive breeding programs are increasing the numbers of animals.
2. Answers will vary.
3. Answers will vary. Possible answers include: (1) Make a vegetable or flower garden. (2) Don't litter or pollute freshwater areas. (3) Make posters to hang up in school to raise awareness in others. (4) Leave things in the wild alone and respect their habitats.

Amphibians Crossword Puzzle (p. 38)

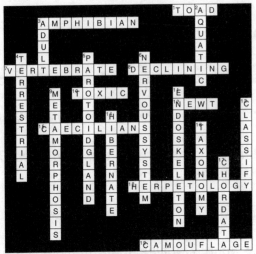

Amphibian Jeopardy (p. 39–40)

1. vertebrate
2. endoskeleton
3. molting
4. the basic needs for all animals
5. skeleton
6. nerve cord (spinal cord)
7. amphibians
8. amphibians lay so many eggs
9. taxonomy
10. herpetologist
11. hibernation
12. ectothermic animals (ectotherms)
13. metamorphosis

14. lobe-finned fish
15. binomial nomenclature
16. (anurans) frogs and toads
17. caecilians
18. salamander
19. toad
20. behavior
21. parotoid glands
22. camouflage
23. bioindicator or biological indicator
24. the stages of metamorphosis
25. tadpole
26. some reasons for amphibian decline
27. causing the disappearance of the
    Cascades frog

Amphibians Unit Test (p. 41)

Multiple Choice:	Matching:
1. b	1. L
2. d	2. M
3. c	3. G
4. b	4. N
5. c	5. J
6. a	6. I
7. d	7. K
8. c	8. F
9. d	9. A
10. b	10. C
	11. D
	12. B
	13. E
	14. O
	15. H

Bibliography

Biggs, Daniel, and Ortleb. *Life Science.* Glenco/McGraw-Hill, 1997.

Clarke, Dr. Barry. *Amphibians/Eyewitness Books.* Alfred A. Knopf, Inc., 1993.

Parker, Bertha Morris. *Toads and Frogs/The Basic Science Education Series.* Row Peterson
     and Co., 1942.

Pollock, Steve. *The Atlas of Endangered Animals.* Facts on File Publications, 1993.

Stidworthy, John. *Reptiles and Amphibians.* Facts on File Publications, 1989.

Strauss, Lisowski. *The Web of Life.* Scott Foresman-Addison Wesley, 2000.

World Book's Young Scientists: Animals. World Book Inc., 1995.